Meadow the Moose

Alaska Spirit Photography © 2015

written by Bonnie J Brummett

Alaska is Amazing Series / Book 1

ISBN-13: 978-1522750529

ISBN-10: 1522750525

In Memory of and Dedicated to my Dad

He taught me that just because I was a girl, it didn't mean I couldn't do everything I wanted.

Meadow the moose lives in Chickaloon, Alaska. She lives at the bottom of Castle Mountain. Meadow is a female moose, called a cow.

Meadow likes to roam around the trails in Chickaloon looking for her friends that live there too!

Look! There's one now! This is Seward, the young seagull. She will be almost 3 years old before she turns white like the adults in her flock. She's getting a snack on the bank of the Matanuska River near the Glenn Highway.

"Hi Seward!" Meadow steps gingerly into the water.

"What's happening, Meadow?" Seward says as she snatches up a tasty morsel out of the water.

"Just getting started on my day. It's so nice I thought I'd make the rounds and say hello to everyone." Maggie says before dipping her nose to take a drink.

Meadow is careful as she walks near the highway, there are cars and trucks that go by her very fast!

As Meadow walks about visiting all her friends, she leaves hoof prints in the mud, sand and snow, they look like this.

On the other side of the highway across from Seward's place, there is a family of Tundra swans. Each year, around October, the swans pass thru Meadow's area heading for their winter home. She doesn't really get to know them, because they stay on the far side of the pond.

Sometimes Meadow would walk thru this yard to see if there was anything good to eat in the garden. Almost always she would go very early in the morning so she never saw the people that live there. She could hear them moving around inside if she came by too late in the morning.

She does know that they have a large yellow dog that would go in the fenced yard because he would bark very loudly. She also knew his name was Yukon, because that's what the people would call him when they wanted him to come in the house. Meadow wasn't afraid of Yukon, even though he seemed very fierce and protective of his home, she knew he couldn't get outside the fence.

Meadow thought she might like to visit with Copper today, the rooster that lived in the same yard as Yukon, so she went around to the back to the chicken coop to see if he was there.

"Hi Copper!" Meadow said to the bright reddish orange bird.

"Hello Meadow! What are you doing on this fine day?" Copper crowed.

"I thought I'd take a walk around and see what everyone was doing." Meadow lowered her huge head down to Copper.

"Well you have a wonderful visit!" Copper crowed, "I'm off to see what Tok and Tetlin are up to. Those Spangled Russian Orloff girls are always getting into trouble. I hope they didn't fly over the fence again!"

"Good luck, Copper! I'll see you again in a few days." Meadow said as she wandered off, munching on birch tree tips as she made her way down the road. She often ate while she was walking along, finding the best things to munch on as she ambled around.

A bit further down the road she spotted Paxson and Palmer the Ptarmigan twins. Sometimes these two would scare her, and she'd jump, because they blended in with the woods and ground so well that she didn't see them!

"My goodness! You two always give me such a fright!" Meadow shook her head at the two ptarmigan. "But it's a good thing that you can't be easily seen, that way you can hide from anything!"

"We know! We know!" the two trilled in unison. "We like to hide!"

Meadow stomped her front hoof and the twins flew off into the thick woods, their wings making a loud thrumming sound as they went. Meadow continued on her daily walk.

Hoonah the Arctic Hare was very upset that
there was very little snow this year. He
changed the color of his fur coat from brown to
white when winter was approaching, so he
could blend in with the snow and not let
anyone see him!

"Meadow!" Hoonah hopped in between her
feet. "It's a very odd winter indeed! Usually by
now I can burrow into snowbanks and hide

from owls and hawks."

"It is strange." Said Meadow, bowing her head to look, so she didn't step on the small hare. "But, I like not having to wade through the deep snow. Makes it easier for me to go around and visit everyone. Even though I have very long legs, it can still be difficult if the snow is too deep."

"I can see that," said Hoonah. "But it's better for me to go on top of the snow to run and run and hop! I can go fast on top of the snow." He then darted off and was gone in a flash of white fur.

It was starting to get dark, so Meadow thought it was time to head back down the mountain and find a place to sleep for the night. With the small amount of snow that had fallen so far this winter, she could find a cozy spot under a spruce tree that had a nice bed of leaves underneath. Pawing at the snow she made a hollow in the ground and settled in. She looked thru the trees at the sun setting and turning the sky to orange and after a huge yawn, she laid her head down and closed her eyes.

Goodnight and sleep well, Meadow!

Moose Facts

Scientific name: Alces alces

Trophic level: Herbivorous

Higher classification: Alces

The moose is the largest of the deer family, reaching up to 7 foot tall at the shoulder and 590 to 1500 pounds, and with an antler spread up to 6 feet or more. They are located in the

Northern Hemisphere, mostly in Alaska, Canada and Europe. They can also be found in the northeastern United States and as far south as the Rocky Mountains in Colorado. Moose shed their antlers in the fall or early winter following the end of the breeding season. These 'sheds' are often used by carvers to make beautiful creations.

The females are called cows, the males are bulls and the babies are calves. Bulls will bellow loudly to attract a mate. They will also come together once a year to rut. This means that the bulls fight one another with their huge antlers and the victor gets to mate with the cows. Cows normally have one baby each year, but are often seen with twins and rarely, triplets. Moose are most active and feed at dawn and dusk, though they can be seen wandering around during the day. They bed down at night in fields or under trees, and unlike horses, they lay down to sleep. Their coat color ranges from light brown to almost black, with lighter markings on the legs and stomach.

Moose do not have teeth in the front of the upper jaw, but they do have twelve sets of broad, flattened teeth at the rear of the mouth, six pairs of molars and six pairs of premolars. They use their tough, thick tongue and lips to strip tree branches of their leaves, which they crush easily with those back teeth. Depending on what part of the country the moose live in, their summer diet can consist of any of the following: willows, trembling aspen, dogwood, maples, white birch, beaked hazelnut and pin cherry. In winter they mainly eat balsam fir. They are also fond of aquatic plants, such as water shield, yellow pond lily and pondweed. Moose will also raid gardens that people have planted and can consume an entire planting in short order.

Moose can be categorized into four different species in North America: the eastern moose (*A. alces americana*), the Shiras moose (*A. alces shirasi*), the Alaskan moose (*A. alces gigas*), and the northwestern moose (*A. alces andersoni*).

Moose have a lifespan of 8-10 years and they are solitary animals. When they do gather together, it's called a herd. They are able to run at speeds up to 35 miles per hour and can swim up to 10 miles without stopping.

Email: alaskaspiritcrafts@gmail.com

Regular Website: http://www.alaskaspiritcrafts.com

Facebook business page:

https://www.facebook.com/pages/Alaska-Spirit-Crafts/324610579984

Facebook personal page:
https://www.facebook.com/Wolfwoman.Alaska

Facebook group:
https://www.facebook.com/groups/rabbitsoffgrid/

Facebook group marketplace:
https://www.facebook.com/groups/ROGFFAFM/

This has been:

Volume 1 of the

Alaska is Amazing Series

Now, if you've really enjoyed reading about Meadow, please go to Amazon and leave a 5-star review for me. For you see, I haven't hired a big, fancy publisher to distribute my books and make me a millionaire – I've done all this myself! So, by leaving a good review, that lets other people know that you love Meadow and her antics and they'll be interested as well, and in going forward, there will be more Alaskan critter books for you to enjoy with your kids!

Next in the Series:

McGrath the Moose:

Alaska is Amazing Series

Book 2

A bit about me….

Sometimes life gets in the way of what you really want to do with it. If you're lucky, as I have been, to be able to live out a lifelong dream, then you are a fortunate individual indeed.

Born and raised in Upstate New York in a fairly rural area, my folks were gardeners more than farmers, and we always had a plethora of fresh veggies through the summer and canned goods lasting thru the winter. Somehow, while that was wonderful, it just was not enough for me. I often would go out in the uncut field behind the garden and just sit and draw or read, and listen. I remember one summer tracking a deer through the woods and into the neighboring farmland. I never did see it, but at the time his hoof print spanned the size of my hand. I was intrigued and fascinated by nature and felt most at peace when by myself in my own little world.

I did dream of living somewhere away from anyone as a hermit – something that I now know was a tad unreasonable, but not totally unattainable. As the years went by and I thought more of this, met others that might feel the same, I knew that it could happen.

I now live in a small, native Alaskan town 30 miles from nowhere. My cabin in the woods is 4 miles off the main road, and it is a dry, off-grid home. I can drive there, though more than a few times I have postponed trips into town due to snow. The old adage "Better safe than sorry" definitely applies! My husband and I currently have 3 large, aging dogs and over 30 rabbits, which provide both meat and fur.

The wild animals that I've seen, photographed and watched have recently inspired me to share some adventures with the younger readers, and that's where this series comes in.

This place can either inspire people to really live the life they have always wanted, or it can crush every hope they have ever had – if you are up to it, as I am sure some of you are, it is well worth everything she throws at you, and the rewards of persevering are more than you have ever dreamed!

Never tell me I can't, because I will!

www.ingramcontent.com/pod-product-compliance
Lightning Source LLC
Chambersburg PA
CBHW050924290526
45792CB00002B/877